C000001289

50 THINGS TO KNOW ABOUT BEING CHILDFREE BY CHOICE

A Guide for Understanding and Acceptance

Kelly Hawkins

Cover designed by: Ivana Stamenkovic
Cover Image: https://pixabay.com/photos/freedom-woman-road-city-happy-2940655/

CZYK Publishing Since 2011.
CZYKPublishing.com
50 Things to Know

Lock Haven, PA
All rights reserved.
ISBN: 9798509457692

50 THINGS TO KNOW ABOUT BEING CHILDFREE BY CHOICE

BOOK DESCRIPTION

Do you hear silence instead of the hands of the mythical biological clock ticking? Does your heart flutter faster when you see a puppy than it does when you see a tiny human? Do you break into a cold sweat when you receive a baby shower or child's birthday invitation? If you answered yes to any of these questions then this book is for you...

50 Things to Know about Being Childfree by Choice, by Kelly Hawkins, offers a candid and humorous description of why she and several other women she interviewed have chosen not to have children. Most books on being childfree tell you about how it is an atypical decision. Although there's nothing wrong with that, and the decision is still not the norm, the number of women and couples that are choosing to lead a life without kids is on the rise. In fact, it is becoming what some would consider a movement.

In these pages you'll discover the various personal experiences, alternative priorities, fears, and challenges that have led the author and some of her closest family and friends to pursue paths other than motherhood. This book will help you understand that being a mom is not a role that every woman desires to play.

By the time you finish this book, you will know why it can sometimes feel lonely as a childfree woman, but will discover that if you too have felt this way, you have a larger support network than you may think. So grab YOUR copy today. You'll be glad you did.

TABLE OF CONTENTS

50 Things to Know About Being Childfree by Choice

DEDICATION

To Marge Burns, Nancy Creed, Katelyn Iacolo, Heather Moffatt, Karissa Venne, Samm Vinesett, and Kelly Williamson, and to Kelly, Megan C., and Carly F. - thank you for sharing your thoughts, reasons, and stories and for making my childfree circle of friends so much larger.

And to my best friend, Ashlea Sarnelli, who despite being an amazing mom to three beautiful children and one perfect angel, has never questioned or judged my choices even though they are vastly different than her own.

ABOUT THE AUTHOR

Kelly Hawkins was born and raised in Western Massachusetts. After transferring from Fairfield University to Bay Path University, she was asked by one of her professors to become a writing and academic tutor for her peers. She enjoyed the work so much, that after graduating Summa Cum Laude, she pursued her Master of Arts in Teaching from Elms College.

She has worked in education for the last twenty-two years, eighteen of which have been as a full time member of the English Department at Agawam High School. During her tenure, Kelly has taught students of all ages and abilities in grades nine through twelve in a variety of core and elective courses. Although she has loved working with other people's children, she and her husband have happily made the decision not to have any of their own. They are quite content and fulfilled with the other children in their lives - students, nieces, nephews, and godchildren - as well as their beloved dog.

In addition to teaching, Kelly has recently completed several freelance writing projects, including contributing posts to *The Hark Journal* – a

3

free email subscription that provides daily inspirational messages for today's world based on Shakespearean quotes. She is also the author of *50 Things to Know about Being a High School English Teacher* and narrated the audiobook version as well. She hopes to continue with freelance writing and complete additional book narrations and voiceover work in the near future.

Please visit any or all of the following to find out more about Kelly Hawkins as a writer and narrator:

Amazon, goodreads, and ACX Narrators

Instagram: @kmo_hawkins

Facebook: www.facebook.com/kellyemhawkins

Website: www.kellyehawkins.com

INTRODUCTION

"I'm completely happy not having children. I mean, everybody does not have to live in the same way. And as somebody said, 'Everybody with a womb doesn't have to have a child any more than everybody with vocal cords has to be an opera singer.'"

\- Gloria Steinem

As a teacher by trade, I have a strong inclination to educate people. The decision to remain childfree is still not widely understood or embraced, at least not in my experience. My goal is to help others better comprehend and perhaps even gain a bit more empathy for those of us that have discovered that we don't wish to procreate. I would love for that choice to become more accepted and not viewed as a negative decision. I also want to provide a resource for women like me to let them know they are not alone.

Writing a book about what it's like to be a childfree woman has been a dream of mine for quite some time. Although it makes us very happy, I sometimes feel isolated because of the choice my husband and I made not to have children. Believing I was in the minority and feeling uncomfortable sharing my thoughts on the subject for fear of being judged or misunderstood, I have avoided fulfilling my aspiration – until now. When the opportunity arose to write a second book (my first was *50 Things to Know about Being a High School English Teacher*), I decided it was time to share my story and the stories of several women that have traveled a similar journey. I reached out to my childfree by choice friends and family to see if any of them would be willing to provide their thoughts, ideas, and experiences. I was overwhelmed with the responses I received. There are many women in my life that desired to share their reasons for not following the path of parenthood. It made me realize that my support network is so much larger than I ever knew. It also illustrated the importance of sharing your truth. It often helps you find others with whom you can connect.

There are quite a few folks out there that don't want children of their own, and the number is steadily increasing. Although there are a myriad of reasons that people choose not to reproduce, and each one is completely valid, it still isn't the "traditional choice." Therefore, a lot of people don't understand women like me that just never had the desire to become a mom. For most females, it seems like the "natural" role they'll fill when they reach a certain age. I never felt that "maternal instinct" or heard the "biological clock" ticking. I've always felt like an outsider when surrounded by so many women that are mothers, but I knew babies would be absent from my future.

There is still such a stigma attached to being childfree by choice. We're seen by some as selfish or cold. Our preference for not having offspring is for some reason considered a negative thing and is sometimes met with a trace of disdain. I hope that by reading the upcoming pages, people will better understand our perspective and view it as what it is – simply a choice that differs from the current majority.

The women I informally interviewed for this book range in age from being in their twenties to their sixties. They consist of family, friends, and former students. Some wanted to remain completely anonymous, further illustrating that certain prejudice still exists around our choices. To respect their wishes and the privacy of those that did allow their names to be included in the dedication, I refer to them in a general manner throughout the book, even when using quotations as to not single out any individual. I want to thank them for their courage, candor, and willingness to share their stories in order to help others feel not so alone.

PRIOR TO READING

The sole purpose of this book is to present my experience and the experiences of others that have made the same choice as me – to be childfree. It is certainly not my intention to upset or offend anyone. Although I have attempted to incorporate humor in some of the pages that follow, I do respect women that have chosen to become moms. I don't understand it, it's not for me, but if it's what makes others happy, I fully support it. I joke about certain situations but don't mean to belittle the role of mothers in any way. It must be a tremendously difficult job and it's an extremely important one – I just don't feel it's *the* most important one, at least not for all of us.

In addition, I want to recognize those people that long to have children of their own but for whatever reason cannot. My wish for them is that they can learn to find happiness in other ways or that by some miracle, their dreams are fulfilled. I also empathize with those that have had an arduous path in having their hopes of becoming parents brought to fruition. I acknowledge and appreciate your journey, even though it is not my own.

PART A: CHILDHOOD EXPERIENCES

1. HAPPY CHILDHOOD

My parents are Dick and Jane. No, seriously, those are their names, so how could I have anything other than an idyllic childhood? Dick and Jane have been married for fifty-six years and have three children – my older brother, my older sister, and yours truly. They also have four grandchildren, none of whom are my progeny.

Not all women that choose to be childfree experienced a negative childhood. Some of us have very happy memories from our early days and feel like we could never live up to the level of nurturing that our mothers and fathers provided. In my house, exceptional parenting appeared to come naturally. My mom and dad always seemed to know what to do. (I know now they didn't perpetually have the right answers, but as a kid I felt as though they did, and that was very comforting.)

My parents were always very present in our lives and still are. They knew how we were doing in school, who our friends were, and when we were struggling with something. We had family dinners each night and they helped with homework whenever we needed it. I recall so many wonderful holidays and birthday parties when we were thoroughly spoiled. (My mom even held my sixth birthday party right after the passing of her own mother, my grandmother. I still don't know how she got through it, but that's the level of sacrifice that my parents followed - whatever it took to make us happy.)

Both my mother and father attended every school play, dance recital, parent-teacher conference, art show, and game for all three of us. I have countless notes and cards from them openly sharing their pride and love for me. (I still have several cherished letters my dad sent to me while I was away at college. He would always include some "pizza money" in them too for his "poor college student" daughter.)

My mom used to read to me before bed. *The Secret Garden* and *Charlotte's Web* were two of my favorites. My dad would often get us small treats whenever we stopped at the store. Mom always knew exactly what to do whenever we got sick. Dad shared his love of old movies with me and we would spend time together watching them. (*Rear Window* with Grace Kelly was one of our favorites.)

I inherited my parents' strict work ethic, their love and appreciation of the arts and literature, and their belief that everyone deserves kindness. I did not, however, receive my mother's proclivity for gardening or my father's talent for painting. And despite the fact that I love my family fiercely and possess an intense fascination of genealogy, I also didn't inherit their desire to add leaves to my family tree.

I know deep in my heart that I don't have what it takes to provide for my own children the kind of childhood that I had. I don't have the energy to run around at the park with kids or the desire to play games with them. I lack the creativity to plan themed birthday parties and make cupcakes from scratch. I don't want to read the same story to a young one night after night when I'm exhausted. It is just not in me.

Both my parents worked hard and made sacrifices to provide a beautiful home, where our friends were always welcomed. I was (and still am) proud to introduce my mom and dad to people. They have been fantastic role models. Life wasn't perfect, but I consider myself very fortunate to have had the childhood I did. I will forever be grateful to the two of them for the incredible job they did raising my siblings and me. My decision to remain childfree has absolutely no reflection on them as parents. I had to follow my heart and forge my own path for happiness, which I've done. It just so happens that my route did not include having kids of my own.

2. NO DOLLS FOR ME!

Looking back, I guess I subconsciously knew from a very early age that I would not be a mother. While my friends were all wishing that Santa would leave them Cabbage Patch dolls under their Christmas trees, I was hoping for more stuffed animals to add to my collection. I found (and still find) dolls to be creepy. I never had the natural inclination to want to feed, clothe, rock, and sing to an inanimate plastic baby. I just didn't understand the point I guess. I never really thought much about it until I began examining my childfree life more closely.

The desire to care for another living thing was definitely there, but I would channel that nurturing instinct into tending to my stuffed animals. I remember dressing my plush Snoopy in different outfits, and nursing my teddy bear back to health. I had a huge collection of fuzzy bears, dogs, cats, and even turtles that resided on my bed. I felt more of a connection to them than any of the few dolls I ever had. I would say goodnight to each of them and get upset if they happened to tumble off the bed. I guess my heart has just always been programmed to react more strongly to animals, even fake ones, than tiny humans – real or fake.

3. BIRTH ORDER

Another aspect that may influence our decision not to procreate is our birth order within the family. As the youngest in my household, I obviously had no little siblings to look after. I didn't have to help take care of anyone else when I was a child. (Interestingly, I have found that being the youngest in the family is a trait that I share with many of the interviewees for this book.) I didn't have a lot of opportunities to interact with kids that were younger than me. I occasionally babysat when I was old enough but mostly just for cousins with whom I was close.

I did work at a kids' camp when I was in my twenties, but that experience probably helped to clinch my "no kids" decision. It took so much energy to look after the teenage counselors as well as the little campers that were placed in my care. "Camp Buckaroo" was the morning session, and "Camp

Scamperoo" was the afternoon session. (Insert eye roll here.) We were supposed to have a lunch break in between, but parents would inevitably pick their kids up late and drop them off early, so there was always an overlap. Between removing splinters, flushing sand from the sandbox out of eyes, creating and monitoring daily arts and crafts projects, preparing snacks, and taking care of accidents – even though all campers were *supposedly* potty-trained – helped to seal my fate. That is not what I saw myself doing in the days to come.

4. UNHAPPY CHILDHOOD

I realize that I was lucky in my circumstances and not everyone is fortunate enough to be raised in happy families. Some people avoid having children because they experienced a very difficult or even traumatic childhood. Perhaps they lived in a home where there was physical, emotional, or verbal abuse. Maybe money was tight, tensions were high, and their parents constantly argued. Sadly, they may have been lacking a loving and supportive environment, and it's no guarantee that they had both parents with them in the home which makes things even more challenging.

Children of divorce sometimes choose not to have kids. They fear the same thing that happened to their parents could happen to them, repeating history. One friend shared with me that both she and her partner come from broken homes, and they each watched their single mothers struggle. That experience has discouraged them from having children of their own. We all hope that when we enter a relationship with someone that it will last, but that's not always the case. Splitting up is a real possibility for any couple, and when children are involved, it's all the more taxing. The thought of suddenly trying to raise children independently and possibly not being able to adequately provide for them is frightening. That fear can often be enough to prevent people from wanting to start a family.

5. LIMITED CHILDHOOD

Sometimes experiences of being a child are not particularly positive or negative, but they simply don't last as long as one would've envisioned. A number of different circumstances can force some kids to have to grow up faster than normal. Occasionally parents or guardians become ill, and the children prematurely develop into their caretakers. This level of adult responsibility is difficult to handle and robs children of many typical experiences that their peers have. This enormous weight being placed on one's shoulders at an early age can make a person avoid having children, fearing the same thing may happen again. They don't want to ever have to place that burden on their own children because they know first-hand how challenging it is.

As a way to make up for lost time, some couples that had childhoods such as these may choose to live their lives with youthful spirits and participate in the activities that they missed out on when they were young. I know a few couples like this. One pair was never able to take family vacations in their youth, so they decided to visit Disneyland themselves.

Another couldn't afford to have pets when they were little, so now they have several animals that they spend their time and money on instead of children. They thoroughly enjoy each other's company as partners, have a great deal of fun together, and that's more than enough for them.

PART B: OTHER PEOPLE'S KIDS

6. NIECES AND NEPHEWS

I would suspect that I've felt fulfilled through the years, not only thanks to the love of my family, husband, friends, and dogs, but because I do have plenty of children in my life - they just aren't mine.

One of my favorite roles is that of auntie. My brother and sister-in-law have a daughter that many have said is my "mini-me." When we're out together, it's often assumed that I'm her mother. (We always get a good chuckle out of those assumptions due to the irony of the situation.) Although I've always loved her and enjoyed spending time with her, now that she's a teenager, I feel that I understand her better. I can relate to her more now than when she was a toddler. I'm comfortable interacting with her because as a high school teacher, I'm used to her age group. We can have conversations about all kinds of topics. Her parents have done an incredible job raising her. She is an amazingly well-rounded and special young lady. She's one of the people in my life with whom I am the closest. I would do anything for her, yet she is not mine.

My sister and brother-in-law have three children. They live much farther away, so we don't tend to see them as often. However, I can still recall how excited I was every time we received the phone call once each baby had arrived. I couldn't wait to tell my friends that I was an auntie again. I love to see pictures and videos of them. I enjoy hearing stories about them, and I certainly have cherished their visits through the years.

I must reiterate, I love them dearly, but one visit in particular with my sister and her family only solidified that I knew I didn't want the responsibility of having my own offspring. I had taken the train to see them. A few days later, we made the road trip back home in her car, which took several long hours. At the time, she only had two children, one a toddler and one an infant. The little electric toy that she had gotten for her daughter stopped working the moment we hit the road, so there wasn't a whole lot other than the CD of children's songs to distract her. After listening to that on repeat, with my nephew's crying as the chorus, my nerves were a bit frayed. I remember leaping from the car in the driveway as soon as we reached my parents' house, relieved to have my freedom back, thinking, "I love them, but nope! I don't want that." (By the way, as soon as we arrived at our destination, my niece's toy started working again.) The truth is I would love to take a road trip with my sister and her family now. She and her husband have raised three kind, intelligent, and hilarious human beings. The only tears that may appear this time would be from excessive laughter.

We also have several nieces and nephews on my husband's side of the family. Again, we love them all very much and look forward to seeing them at holiday and birthday gatherings. They're great kids and have grown up way too fast. However, after a few hours of laughing, playing, running around, opening presents in a frenzied flurry of wrapping paper, and consuming copious amounts of pizza and cake, my husband and I are happy to return to our quiet house, where we don't have anyone to look after, except the dog.

We love each and every one of our nieces and nephews. We just also love the choices we have made. We can have fun with them, spoil them, and then... go home. We have the best of both worlds.

7. FRIENDS' CHILDREN

Similarly to our nieces and nephews, we love our friends' children as well. We're even the godparents to my best friend and her husband's daughter. When people I am close with announce that they're expecting a baby, I'm genuinely happy for them. I don't understand that desire, but I certainly don't judge it, criticize it, or begrudge what brings them joy. I also admit I do have fun picking out baby gifts, as long as it's not clothing - but more on that later. I enjoy visiting with them and holding their babies before they can walk or talk. If I love you, I love your kids.

8. STRANGERS' OR AQUANTAINCES' CHILDREN

I'm going to be brutally honest here - when I encounter the offspring of strangers or mere acquaintances, that's when the disconnect happens. If I don't know you well, I don't particularly want to see the seventy-two most recent pictures of your litter. If we're not family or very close friends, I'll definitely not be offended if you omit my name from the invitation list to your baby shower. I can think of a great many things I would much rather do on a beautiful weekend afternoon than watch someone open one hundred and seven gifts that everyone "oooohhhss" and "aaahhhhhssss" over if we aren't that close. For example, baby shoes don't make my heart flutter. Instead, I ask myself, "Why on earth does a newborn need shoes?" I know that this makes me sound heartless. I'm really not. These things just don't interest me if I don't have a bond with you. I guess I'm wired differently than most women.

I've also been in more than one uncomfortable situation at work over the years where my preference to not be around kids that I have no connection with has surfaced. We have about twenty-six minutes from bell to bell to eat lunch at school. By the time my classroom clears out, I walk down to the teachers' lounge, use the restroom (if there's not a line), and settle in to eat, half my lunch time is already gone. On several occasions, colleagues have excitedly come for a visit with their new babies. Again, I'm honestly happy for you, but I've always been the only woman there that doesn't spring out of her seat and race to wash her hands so she can hold the infants. The children are usually passed around the lunch table like the Lion King and fawned over. Inevitably, when the little cub reaches me, I just hold my hands up and quietly say, "Nah, I'm good" and resume eating my tuna sandwich. My best friend who obviously knows me well thinks these encounters are hilarious, but I imagine that I come off as cold and callous to some other people in the room. That is my truth though – I'm just not that fascinated by children, unless they are those of family or friends.

PART C: ALTERNATIVE PRIORITIES

9. CAREER

Some of the childfree by choice women that I interviewed shared that they have alternative priorities to motherhood. A great number of them love their careers and they can't imagine making them any less of a focus in their lives. They're able to work longer hours or have a more flexible schedule, because they don't have to worry about when the daycare closes or missing the soccer game. One friend honestly shared that she would not have the time or energy to spend with children once she finally does return home at the end of each day. She's a fantastic chef and works ten to thirteen hour shifts. She knows that for her personally there's no way that she'd be up for taking care of little ones after working that many hours. Another young lady I know is a zoo keeper. Her schedule requires her to work weekends and holidays and possibly even travel the country. That's a big factor in her wish to remain childfree.

Many of us are thrilled by the fact that after working all day, we can return to a kid-free zone at night and relax in peace and quiet. I give credit to working parents. To spend hours at a demanding job and then come home and have the responsibility to care for others is not something I'd enjoy. I decided to give my all to my vocation, which is to care for and educate other people's children. By the time I get home, I usually have nothing left to give.

10. CHILD-CENTERED JOBS

I've worked in education for the last twenty-two years. I refer to my students as my kids, because I spend more time with some of them than their own families do. I attend their plays, concerts, and games. I celebrate their successes and support them during their failures. I worry about some of them at night and long after they've been in my classroom. I certainly believe that I've channeled any "maternal instinct" that may be present in me into my teaching career.

Inevitably it will come up during the school year that my husband and I don't have any kids. The majority of my students are always shocked by this news. They've told me things such as, "You have that 'mom vibe.' I just assumed you had kids of your own." A few years ago, a student had my favorite reaction to date. She asked, "Really? You don't have kids?" and then continued, "That's surprising. I picture you driving around in a mini-van and being the 'soccer mom' that brings orange wedges to your kids and their friends at practice." Several students have shared that they consider me to be their "school mom," and one young lady very sweetly revealed one day, "I wish you were my mom."

I truly appreciate these comments. I'm happy to know I've played a role in many kids' lives, but not a starring one. When I go home for the day, I don't have to help anyone with their homework. I don't have to make anyone chicken nuggets or mac and cheese or drive anyone to ballet lessons. I can watch TV or read. I can even take a nap, which I often do. I love those aspects of my life. Working with other people's children has brought me a great deal of joy, but I'm also thankful that they're not my responsibility every minute of every day.

Many of the women I interviewed prefer to care for children that are not theirs. In addition to teaching, there are a large number of jobs that center around kids that those of us without any may have and enjoy. I have a friend that is an excellent OBGYN nurse. She loves babies, but she simply doesn't want any of her own. Some other jobs that involve working with children include: social workers, pediatric nurses, pediatricians, bus drivers, child psychologists, and nannies. There are also jobs that provide opportunities to work with children on occasion, if that is your preference, such as barbers, librarians, and museum curators. There are plenty of ways in which to interact, care for, and teach children if you wish, and they don't have to share your genes.

11. SIGNIFICANT OTHERS

Along with careers taking the top priority in some women's lives, several fellow childfree friends divulged that they would prefer to concentrate on the relationships between them and their significant others, rather than with any children. A close friend of mine reveals that she intends to keep her life small, simple, and focused on her partner and herself. Her preference is to cultivate that special relationship between the two of them. Having children would certainly impact and alter that bond. Another woman explains, she *chose* to love her husband and he doesn't literally need her to take care of his well-being. The intense and constant obligation of caring for another human is not present, and she prefers it that way. She and her husband are able to spend a great deal of quality time together doing the activities they both enjoy without the constant responsibility of caring for children.

Whatever your romantic life looks like, I think it's extremely important to have an honest conversation with any potential significant other early in the relationship. You must be upfront with your partner when it comes to not wanting to bear children. In a perfect world, you would both be in complete agreement that parenting is not for either of you. Sometimes, however, it can work if one member of a couple decides that they can truly be content without children, because that's what their partner desires. They make a sacrifice for the one they love, yet can find happiness and peace with their decision.

Some of my other friends just never met people they felt strongly enough about to share their lives with permanently, or they knew their former partners couldn't be the type of parents that they envisioned for their children. Therefore, they decided against following the parenthood journey. A few that never met the right person briefly considered adoption or surrogacy, but the more they contemplated the challenges of being single parents, they opted not to pursue those routes. They shared that they're perfectly fine with that. They have no regrets and are satisfied living a childfree life.

12. ADDITIONAL PERSONAL RELATIONSHIPS

In addition to putting energy into the relationships with their partners, many women without kids put a great deal of time and effort into their other personal connections as well. That's not to say that parents don't do the same thing, but those of us without youngsters may have more time to dedicate to people such as our own parents.

I place a very high value on the relationships in my life - my family members, friends, colleagues, students, and former students. I enjoy caring for others; I just don't want to do it with my own brood.

My position as the childfree sibling in my family has provided me the opportunities to assist my parents as they age. My brother and sister both help as well, but being the one without the responsibility of kids, I'm able to be there more often. I attempt to solve Mom and Dad's issues with technology. I frequently stop by for visits on the patio and call them several times a week to check in to see how they are or if they need anything. I recognize that my close proximity also enables me to do this, but it's really that my schedule is more open and flexible. I'm able to bring my mom to a doctor's appointment or go for a walk with my dad.

As a childfree teacher with a summer vacation, my level of freedom also allowed me to assist my folks when they decided to downsize, leaving the home they had lived in for forty-six years. That was an incredibly daunting task, but we got it done. Again, my brother and his family, my sister and her family, my husband, additional relatives, and some wonderful neighbors of my parents helped with this monumental undertaking as well, but I was the one with the most time to spend there to complete the move and all that went with it.

I love that I've had these chances to be there for my mom and dad. As previously mentioned, they provided all of us with amazing childhoods. I'm grateful that I can repay a very small part of what they gave to me. I can offer them a level of support and care that I know I wouldn't be able to if I had kids of my own. I would do anything for them – except provide them with grandchildren. The only thing they will ever get from me and my husband are "grand pups," and they have graciously accepted this fact.

13. PETS

My childfree friends and I obviously have a lot in common, but one trait in particular stands out: we have, adore, and spoil animals. Many people without kids devote a great deal of time to their pets and spend a small fortune on them. We tend to fulfill any maternal (or paternal) instincts with our cats and dogs, rabbits and reptiles instead of infants.

In speaking to my friends that do have children, being a pet owner is similar to having kids in some ways, just on a smaller scale. We too care for a living being. We pay for their food, necessary supplies, medications, treats, and toys. We guide them and teach them right from wrong. We must ensure our pets get enough exercise, play-time, and socialization. Both pets and children do better having an established routine, and they always require supervision. When we can't be there for them, we must provide a trusted caretaker.

I would imagine that some of the frantic phone calls I've placed to the vet over the years about concerns I've had when our dogs were puppies or not feeling well, would sound fairly close to a mother speaking with her child's pediatrician. I've worried about our pets' health, happiness, well-being, and longevity. Historically, our dogs have always come with us on vacations, and we end up packing just as much for them as for ourselves, or so it seems. We've always tried to take the very best care of our pups and consider them family members. When they pass, it can be just as painful as it is with some humans we've lost. (I realize only certain people will understand that statement, and that's OK. If you know, you know.) The love I have for our dogs is more than enough for me. I don't need children to feel fulfilled, and many of my childfree friends agree.

PART D: FREEDOM

14. SLEEP

One of the biggest reasons that I'm thankful that my husband and I decided not to have children is that we have more control over our sleep schedule. He's an early riser and likes to get up and dive into his day. My natural clock keeps me up late. I find that I do my best work well into the night, so whenever I can, I prefer to sleep in to feel that I'm getting an adequate amount of rest. I also don't sleep that well, as I have a difficult time shutting my mind off before going to bed. When I have a poor night's sleep, it definitely affects my mood. It can make me irritable or feel foggy. However, I often have the option of sneaking in a late afternoon nap, which is a luxury I never take for granted.

Acquiring adequate slumber was a very popular reason among the interviewees as to why they too are childfree. One woman shared, "Sleep is definitely a big one for me. When I'm overtired, there is a deep melancholy that sets in." The importance of sleep is often overlooked. It plays such a large role in our physical and mental health. Getting enough quality rest allows us to perform at our optimal level.

Along with being one of the most popular, I feel like this reason is one for which we are most judged. I think a lot of folks consider "sleeping in" to be a trait of laziness. The idea of sacrificing sleep as being honorable has become the norm in society. It almost feels like a competition some days. We reward depriving ourselves of what we need as though it's a positive action. I'd love to see this mindset shift somehow. While I realize that having children inhibits parents from getting enough quality sleep, I wish it didn't. I also hope that someday those of us without kids are not viewed as lazy or selfish just because we may spend more time in our jammies.

15. HOBBIES/VOLUNTEER WORK

Another perk to not having kids is we have more time to pursue our interests outside of work. If we want to watch a movie uninterrupted, we can – unless the dog barks. Once the dog is fed, walked, and has gone out, I can go upstairs to my home office, shut the door, and write for a few hours, without the responsibility of having to care for a dependent being. My husband is a big soccer fan. He doesn't have to watch cartoons and kids' shows when he doesn't feel like it; he can just change the channel to watch a match whenever there is one on TV. I have the freedom to read as many chapters of a book as I want on a random weekend afternoon. I can go for a long walk by myself if I choose. Having the ability to do the things that bring me joy is very important to me and helps keep me balanced.

Being without children also allows some of us to have a more flexible schedule, so we can donate our time more easily to selected charitable causes. We can stay at events longer, because we don't have the same pressing responsibilities waiting for us at home. We don't have to relieve a babysitter or rush to a basketball game. It's yet another example of freedom in our lives that we fully appreciate.

This is not to say that people with children don't spend time volunteering or giving to charities – they absolutely do. Often, you see entire families contributing their time helping others, which is wonderful. I just imagine it's trickier to find time in a more demanding family schedule than it is if you're childfree.

16. SOCIAL OPPORTUNITIES

A lighter schedule also allows us to more easily accept social invitations. When the opportunity arises, if my husband and I feel like attending, we can just go. We don't have to worry about arranging and paying a babysitter. (We're very fortunate that if we will be gone somewhere for more than a few hours that my in-laws will come over to care for the dog.) If we decide to go out to dinner at the last minute, we can, hassle-free. We don't have to be concerned about getting home before a child's bedtime or experience anxiety about how things are going when we aren't there. It's another form of autonomy that we relish.

17. TRAVEL

Many of my childfree friends mentioned that their love of traveling is another consideration that's impacted their choices. They can easily pick up and go wherever they want to - provided they have the financial means to do so. They don't have to worry about taking kids out of school to go on a family vacation or otherwise disrupting their children's routine. One friend admitted that she would rather spend her hard-earned money on traveling and gaining new experiences than paying for any children's needs.

Another young woman shared that she would not only like to travel, but she's also hoping to be able to live in various locations throughout her life. She doesn't wish to be tied down to one specific place. However, she recognizes that it's important to raise children with a certain level of stability. She's following her dreams but is also thinking about what's best for kids. She knows that both things could not coincide in her life, so after this thoughtful process, she's made the decision that's right for her.

PART E: FINANCIAL REASONS – KIDS ARE *REALLY* EXPENSIVE!

18. PRIOR TO ARRIVAL

While conducting my interviews, I found the financial aspect to resonate with many of the women in my childfree circle. If things were different, and they did desire children, several of them feel that their current incomes would never allow them to care for and support a family at the level they would wish.

Repeated Amazon deliveries will arrive at your doorstep well before the stork, as the credit card bill steadily increases. The pregnancy tests and the prenatal vitamins usually start the ball rolling. There are not only the necessities that need to be purchased, but the luxuries if folks are able to afford them. Expectant mothers need maternity clothes, supportive shoes, pillows to try to get more comfortable at night, and the antacids for the horrible heartburn from which they are most likely suffering. Hopefully they have good insurance for all of the pregnancy health care visits and ultrasounds. (I can't even imagine the medical bills that accompany pregnancies with complications or that require surgery.)

Mommies-to-be may want books about baby care and choosing names or desire to have a maternity photoshoot, which if you're on any sort of social media, you know have become quite popular.   Not to mention the "extras" like a humongous water bottle to ensure proper hydration, comfy robes and slippers, massage cushions, or the special hair serum and face and body creams that I've never even heard of and don't really want to know what they're supposed to do.

There are a plethora of items that should be acquired before the bun pops out of the oven such as a stroller, crib, and the proper car seat, (and perhaps even a larger vehicle in which to fit said car seat or have room for future siblings). Let's not forget the diapers, wipes, bottles, pacifiers, baby clothes, blankets, playpens, high chairs, crib sheets, bumper guards, baby bath tubs, skin-sensitive soaps and creams, baby food, and a baby monitor or two. These are all things that are needed (or wanted) even before the kid takes their first steps!

19. INFANTS/YOUNG CHILDREN

Once these small humans are mobile, the need for cabinet locks, baby gates, and plug covers emerges. Their miniature hands and mouths require tiny spoons, forks and sippy cups. They now need a booster car seat, and of course, more clothes and shoes, as they seem to outgrow things by the day. I feel like, at least when they're still young, you can get away with not going overboard with the birthday and holiday gifts, because they don't know any better. (Is that just me?)

When you do have the need or want to go out without them, you must get a reliable babysitter. If you have trusted family or friends that will watch your offspring for free, you're very fortunate. Having to pay someone to care for your child for a few hours is expensive enough. Constant daycare if both parents work must be astronomical, if you can even find an open spot.

As the years progress, you continue to watch your money get spent as quickly (or more quickly) than you make it. After all, kids continue to require food, clothing, and medical care but now you add on things like lunchboxes, school supplies, and backpacks. Sporting equipment, uniforms, dance lessons, and musical instruments will also help to empty your wallet. And now, not only do you have to buy gifts to celebrate their birth, but the births of all of their little friends too.

Depending on your religion and culture, things like Halloween costumes (unless you're crafty and can make them yourself), Christmas presents from Santa, and baskets from the Easter bunny all add up. Don't forget one of the strangest traditions, in my humble opinion: having your children leave the baby teeth that fall out of their faces under their pillow at night so a magical fairy can leave them money. (OK, I admit, I used to get excited for this ritual when I was a kid too. It just seems much creepier to me now that I look at it as an adult with no kids.) Perhaps religious rites of passage such as Baptisms or First Communions and the parties that follow these events are yet another expense. The list of ways to spend money on children is infinite.

20. TEENAGERS

When I asked my sister what their biggest expense is in a house with three kids as they age she frankly replied, "Food, food, and more food!" She swears their grocery bills quadrupled when her kids hit the teen years. (Ah, to have a working metabolism...)

While many of the same necessities as when they were little still exist, now there are several additions. Raising a teenager in today's society requires quite a few technological items so they will not be left behind. Phones, computers, internet access, and video games are just a few things that come to mind.

Driving lessons, the price of a license, and insurance come into play. Costs for academic assessments such as the SATs, ACTs, or AP exams sneak into your bank statement. Yearbook purchases, college visits, and exorbitant application fees suddenly pop up in your checkbook.

If teenagers have part time jobs that can help to defray the cost of some of these things I'm sure it helps a tad. However, with the low minimum wage, the competition for work, and the increased cost of everything, it probably seems as though it barely makes a dent in the monthly bills.

21. COLLEGE

If your children choose to attend higher education, you're in my thoughts and prayers. I can't even wrap my head around how expensive a college education is today, especially considering that most parents are probably still paying off (or maybe just recently paid off) their own outrageous college loans. Also, a great many parents have more than one child. It makes me cringe just thinking about those loan payments, even with the blessing of things like partial scholarships and financial aid.

22. GRANDCHILDREN

The cycle of spending money on kids is incessant for some people. Once their own children are grown, all of a sudden, grandchildren most likely appear. Often, there are more grandchildren than children, so the purchasing continues!

I will concede the relationship between grandparents and grandchildren is a unique bond. I can recall my own grandparents faithfully sending cards, buying gifts, coming to visit, and giving my siblings and me money on all sorts of different occasions. They exuded kindness and generosity. They were very special people, and I miss having them in my life.

I've also seen the way my own parents spoil their grandchildren. Granted, they're not directly responsible for providing all of the above mentioned items for their grandkids, but what they do buy still adds up. They tend to get the more fun things and luxuries if they can.

Some grandparents also become caretakers all over again if their kids have to go to work and they can't afford day care. That's a wonderful way to spend time with your grandkids, but again, not the choice for me or many others.

PART F: FEARS

23. TOKOPHOBIA

Most people have a severe fear of something – fear of spiders (arachnophobia), fear of clowns (coulrophobia), fear of going outside (agoraphobia) – having a fear of pregnancy and childbirth is no different. The condition is called tokophobia. Although I didn't previously know the term, a former student of mine brought it to my attention. Many women, including me, avoid pregnancy due to the fear of the torture of labor and bearing a child. I just don't have the desire to put myself through that level of voluntary physical pain, no matter the result. It honestly terrifies me.

I also don't like to consider all of the physical discomfort that comes with the lengthy pregnancy before-hand. Being uncomfortable is bad enough when it's beyond one's control. I try to avoid it at all costs. Having to endure the physical repercussions is another major sacrifice that mothers are willing to make, and I commend them for it. I just don't want to personally experience any of it.

24. PHYSICAL TOLL

Becoming pregnant is a life-altering event physically, emotionally, financially, and socially. The physical toll it takes on a woman's body is reason enough for some to avoid going down the child-bearing path. The morning sickness, swollen feet/legs, back pain, excessive urination, discomfort sleeping, and extreme fatigue is just the beginning, and these things occur even when a woman is in very good health. To all of this, I say a hearty, "No, thank you!"

I don't even want to get into the weight gain and some of the severe problems that can develop, such as gestational diabetes and preeclampsia. Bed rest is also a result for a number of pregnant women that I have known due to high-risk pregnancies and unexpected complications.

Just hearing about the labor experiences of some of my family and friends - the pain, exhaustion, and length of time that they were in labor – has been enough to reassure myself that I most definitely have made the correct decision.

25. EMOTIONAL/MENTAL TOLL

I know, as someone that lives with anxiety, I would continuously worry about every little thing from conception until… well, the end of time. And I mean *every* little thing (and medium thing and big thing for that matter.) I would be the world's worst pregnant woman. I'd have my doctor's office on speed dial. They would knowingly roll their eyes when they answered the phone and heard my frantic voice on the other end – again. I'd worry about things that were happening. I'd fret about things that were not happening. I would keep myself up at night creating the worst case scenarios in my head. (You can probably tell by now, I'm one of those "what if" people, but not in the good way.) Some parents-to-be are the optimistic "what iffers." They ponder questions like, "What if our child becomes the

President of the United States?" or "What if our child ends up discovering the cure for cancer?" I can be found at the opposite end of the spectrum: "What if my child is born with some physical ailment that the medical staff has never seen before?" or "What if my child is the one that drives their teachers crazy?" All of this incessant – and I am fully aware, unnecessary – worrying would be before the kid even got here.

The impending sleep deprivation would certainly affect my mood and ability to function properly. The possibility of post-partum depression emerging is all too real. Going through the rest of my life constantly agonizing about the safety, happiness, and well-being of my children does not appeal to me. I can't fathom the fear that strikes parents when they're momentarily separated from their child who wandered off in the grocery store. I don't want to spend a sleepless night tossing and turning when my kid first gets their license and is a few minutes late for curfew. These are not things I dream of doing, and I certainly would not want to hand down this level of anxiety to anyone else.

26. FAMILY HISTORY OF ILLNESS

Perpetuating a trait such as anxiety isn't the only fear some women have when they decide not to have children. They may also have a family history of other mental or physical illnesses or conditions that they refuse to pass on to their kids, even if it's only a possibility. It could be bi-polar disorder, schizophrenia, Alzheimer's, or dementia. It could be diabetes, asthma, cystic fibrosis, or cancer. There may also be a concern of continuing the pattern of substance abuse or addictive tendencies. There are so many ailments a person can have, some a great deal more severe than others.

Numerous childfree women I know have some of these conditions themselves. For instance, a large number of us suffer from not only anxiety but depression as well. We struggle with this reality on a daily basis and some days it can be overwhelming. To add a child into this mix could be detrimental. As mentioned above, post-partum depression is a huge concern of mine, as it is for several of my friends. I know how difficult it is to be in a depressive state. It's challenging enough when you're not responsible for caring for another living being. I can't envision getting through some of my darkest days with the added obligation of having to constantly care for a baby or child. Similar to many other conditions, depression is very difficult to explain to others that don't suffer from it, so I feel that my child wouldn't fully understand my behavior. That would be painful and create a heavy sense of guilt.

Illness is not the only thing that some of us are fearful to pass on to children. Another source of worry for some women that avoid becoming mothers is that they wouldn't want a child that was like they were. One friend shared with me, "I was a challenging personality growing up. My mother would always say when she was angry, 'I hope you have a child like you one day,' and she didn't mean it as a compliment."

Let's face it, kids can (and do) inherit both the positive and the negative traits of their parents. People cannot pick and choose which characteristics their offspring will have. There's a very good possibility that if you were a difficult child growing up, your own children may be the same way or even worse. (There's also a chance that they may be better, but some women I know are not willing to take that gamble). They feel remorse for what they put their parents through and they wouldn't want to experience it themselves.

27. INADEQUACY

Another fear for some of the women that were interviewed is the feeling of inadequacy, especially when they imagine having a child with physical or mental challenges. We can't know for certain how we would act in hypothetical situations, but again, this is a real consideration for some childfree women. The trepidation of not being able to emotionally handle or properly care for a child with special needs is yet another reason for some of us choosing not to have children. The challenges with being a mother to any child are extreme; consider the added layers of stress and responsibilities having a child that needed even more care emotionally or physically, not to mention financially would bring. Parents of children with special needs deserve praise. It can't be an easy journey. I admire you, support you, and empathize with you.

28. CAN'T EVEN TAKE CARE OF MYSELF

A common rationale that kept coming up with the younger women I interviewed was that on some days, they feel like it's a big enough struggle to care for themselves properly; they can't fathom having to tend to a baby. Due to a number of the above stated reasons, they find it challenging to get what they themselves need. They spend long days at work but earn wages that don't reflect that dedication. They most likely have their own school loans to pay off. They may be saving for their first home or making improvements to the one they have. They simply don't feel prepared to provide for another life. They seem trapped in this pattern of work, bills, and time. They don't see an escape in the near future. One friend asked, "How on earth do I get to a point where I can financially and emotionally provide for another life?" She went on to say, "My home is nowhere near ready to bring a baby into, nor can I afford to update it quickly enough to race my body before it becomes unfit to carry a child." Another woman honestly shared, "I don't like the prospect of spending the next eighteen plus years focusing on bringing up one life when I still want to focus on getting a grip on my own."

I give these women credit. They've been thoughtful and careful about their decisions to remain childfree. While some may view this thinking as selfish, I view it as having the knowledge that they couldn't care for a child at the level which they would like, so they decide against it. To me, that exhibits a certain kind of altruism.

29. FEAR OF THE WORLD

Several of my childfree friends have mentioned that they have no desire to bring children into the world in its current state. Although that may sound pessimistic, and there are always challenges within any time period, I wholeheartedly agree with this rationale. Just by watching the news, looking on-line, or reading the newspaper, you witness what a tumultuous time we're experiencing. There's so much hatred, discrimination, injustice, and violence present on our planet. We're currently attempting to survive an unimaginable global pandemic. Some of us don't want to contribute to overpopulation or further negatively influence climate change.

There are an infinite number of wonderful things about the world also. Many people exhibit kindness, acceptance, empathy, and love. There are countless positive influences a child could have and a myriad of amazing aspects of life to which they could be exposed. There's a good chance that the children we would bear may make it a better place, but the world could also work against them. That possibility is enough for us to forego having them. I already have a difficult enough time witnessing the world being unkind to others; I don't think my heart could handle watching that happen to my own flesh and blood.

30. OUTSIDE INFLUENCES

Not only could the world at large negatively affect children, but the harmful influences could be much closer. I've known excellent parents that were attentive, caring, and understanding. They provided lovely homes for their kids and attended their hockey games and band concerts. They put their all into being model parents, and they succeeded, yet their children were overtaken by outside forces that their moms and dads just couldn't control.

One can do "all the right things" as a parent, relatively speaking, but then some friends or significant others come along and have a stronger hold over your child. All of a sudden, they're heading down the wrong path, and there's seemingly nothing you can do to stop it. You can try your best, but when someone doesn't want to be helped, they can't be.

Again, this may seem like an extreme view, but I've witnessed the pain of some parents that have experienced this situation. Just the possibility of it happening scares me enough to ensure that it doesn't.

31. PERMANANCE

The final fear that a few of us share is the permanent nature of becoming a parent. Unlike a car, you can't "test drive" an infant. You can't sign up for a free trial of parenthood as you do an Audible subscription. Once you make this enormous decision that will alter literally every aspect of your life – you're in it for good. There's no turning back. You can't "cancel at any time" or "ask for a full refund" if it doesn't pan out as you expected. Even when people give their children up for adoption, they still created that life; they're still mothers and fathers, and they will hold those titles for the rest of their days.

Although I'm not a huge fan of change, the idea of being trapped in certain situations makes me very uncomfortable. I transferred when I was in college, because I was miserable at my original choice. I switched schools after my initial year of teaching, because the first was not a good fit. Many major life events haven't worked out the first time around for me. Like Goldilocks, I've experienced some hardships before getting it "just right." There's no dress rehearsal or dry run to be a parent. That's too much pressure for a control freak perfectionist like me to handle. You're dealing with another human's life, and they are yours… forever. Yikes!

PART G: ASSUMPTIONS

32. "YOU'LL CHANGE YOUR MIND"

There are many ignorant assumptions that people make pertaining to all kinds of topics. When I was younger, the most common statement that a few individuals I know (and some strangers) made to me with this grandiose authority was, "You say you don't want children, but you'll change your mind!" I would have loved to have replied, "You have no idea how I feel, what I'm thinking, what my reasons are for not wanting children, and you don't even know me that well. Why would you ever say that to someone?" However, I usually changed the subject and moved along with my day.

Voicing that assumption ranks right up there with asking a woman how much she weighs or saying to a child that is significantly younger than her siblings, "Oh, so you were an 'oopsie baby!'" People never cease to amaze me with the words that spill out of their mouths before their brain proofreads them. When you do tell uncouth folks such as these that you have no interest in procreating, some just flat out refuse to believe you so this is their "go to" comment. It apparently makes them more comfortable that my decision not to have children will inevitably change. I must eventually come to my senses and reproduce, right? Then all will be right with the world – their world not mine. Some people simply will not accept that others, women in particular, have no interest in breeding. I'm so sorry to burst these folks' archaic belief bubbles, but not all females want to be moms.

33. MALE PERSPECTIVE

Not all males dream of becoming dads either, but the interactions they have are different. Even though my husband and I have most of the very same reasons for choosing to be childfree, his experience has been quite unlike mine. Granted, he works in an office with a few people, and I work in a school with a staff of over one-hundred, but the same expectations are definitely not placed upon us.

Shortly after we were married, one of the few times the topic of us not having children came up for

him at work. A co-worker said to him, "Just wait…
your wife will want kids before long." First of all, no,
I will not, sir. Second, I don't even know this man
well. Third, why do so many people make this
assumption? Fourth, he never said anything about my
husband changing his mind.

A close friend shared with me a bizarre
repeated assumption that others have made about her
and her husband, also demonstrating a severe double
standard. She told me that whenever her husband
tells people that he doesn't have children, the
common supposition is that, as the woman, she must
have children from a previous marriage or
relationship. What?!? People are so strange.

34. "YOUR BIOLOGICAL CLOCK MUST BE TICKING"

Either I was born without a biological clock,
or it didn't have all of the proper pieces, or the ticking
of the seconds was so soft that I never even heard it. I
have not ever felt the pressure of having children as

time passes. I think it's apparent by now that being a mother was not on my radar.

Several of my friends without kids agree. We've simply lived our lives and enjoyed them as they've passed. We don't have to worry about any strict deadline by which to accomplish life goals. We just don't feel that urgency to begin a family as soon as possible or at all for that matter. A young woman I know told me, "I've never felt the sensation of 'baby-fever...' I do love babies, but I love my freedom more." The notion of there being such a thing as a biological clock luckily seems to be fading. I hope someday soon it gets buried with all of the other antiquated beliefs that still pervade our society.

35. "YOU MUST HATE KIDS"

As the quote in the above paragraph illustrates, not all childfree by choice folks dislike kids. Some of us have plenty of children in our lives that we adore and with whom we thoroughly enjoy spending time. Some of us have selected career paths that enable us to work with and help children day in and day out.

Although I've already mentioned that I don't dislike kids, I do admit that there are certain times that I'd prefer not to be around them. If after a long day, my husband and I go out to dinner, being forced to listen to a wailing infant nearby isn't my favorite way to pass the evening. I would much prefer to eat my nachos in peace.

There are some individuals, however, that frankly don't ever enjoy kids. There are quite a few childfree groups on social media, and they have a wide range of members. Some people just have a quiet acceptance that they will not be parents, but others rage with contempt about every encounter they have with a little human. Some friends of mine are on the latter end of the spectrum. One in particular shared, "I detest children. I always have. Even as a kid, I hated kids. They have been a lifelong annoyance, never a bringer of joy." Even though I don't fully agree with her, this is her truth. She's brave enough to share it and owns it. Even though our feelings toward children are not at the same level, I respect her honesty.

36. "WHO WILL CARE FOR YOU IN YOUR OLD AGE?"

Yet another question folks like to ask those of us without offspring is, "But who will take care of you in your old age?" Don't worry; we have options. Many of us have a network of other younger family members that would be willing to help us as we grow older. We have friends and connections of various ages from several areas of our lives. Although my best guess is those that will look after us will be the staff at the nursing home where we'll end out our days like so many other people, even those that have descendants. Just because you procreate, it doesn't guarantee your kids will be the ones to care for you in your golden years. Chances are, they'll be busy with their own families and have limited amount of time to dedicate to your needs. In a perfect world, children would care for their parents and provide what they require, just as their parents did for them, but this is not always the case. I feel confident that I'll be fine without kids, even as the wrinkles, arthritis, and silver hairs increase.

PART H: EXPECTATIONS

37. SOCIETAL EXPECTATIONS

Along with the assumptions that people make, there exist certain expectations as well. Even though things are changing and more people are choosing to be childfree, it's still a relatively new and not fully accepted concept. Those of us that decide not to bear children are still a minority. A former student of mine eloquently wrote, "Many women find fulfillment in the idea of motherhood, and I think it's often considered a rite of passage to adulthood in our society. From a young age, I have always felt at odds with that since I always knew I never wanted to have kids." Even in 2021, there is still this expectancy that most, if not all, women desire to be mothers and those of us that don't fit this mold are made to feel like outcasts.

Having children has typically been the "natural next step" in people's lives throughout history. Electing not to follow that path is still a very foreign concept to many people, and it probably always will be to a certain extent. It can be daunting to continuously go against the grain of what most people expect, but as my refreshingly honest friend shared, "I prefer to live a life that truly makes me happy and isn't influenced by the societal norms." I admire her acceptance and pride in who she is. Although her choices may be different than what the majority of people select, (and expect others to select) she should not be ostracized or judged for that.

38. FAMILIAL EXPECTATIONS

Sometimes the expectations come from a source literally closer to home. Our own families can have a set of values ingrained within them. Often parents presume that they will someday be grandparents. That is the circle of life, is it not? It can be, but is not a requirement for everyone.

The pressure from family members to procreate can stem from many sources. Perhaps the family belongs to a religion where there are strong beliefs about creating a family. People tend to view children as miracles and consider them a blessing – the more you have, the more blessed your life is.

Another factor may be the family ideals that are shaped by culture. More "traditional" (or in some people's views stereotypical) roles may be stressed, such as the male being the primary provider with his source of income and the female being the caretaker of the home and family.

Several of the women I interviewed noticed a distinct difference between the expectations and treatment of them verses their brothers. One woman shares that even though she is the younger sibling, it is she that is automatically expected to continue the family bloodline. Her parents just assume that she will have kids. The same expectation doesn't seem to be present for her older brother. He may have children; he may not.

Another friend relayed to me that while she was growing up, she was not provided with the same opportunities that her brothers were. Her father was a dentist, and even though she spent a great deal of time working in his office and once considered becoming a dentist herself, her father had figured her brother would take over the reins of the family practice. She, like me, entered the field of teaching instead and ended up helping countless children of others throughout her career.

PART I – OUT OF THE LOOP

39. NOTHING TO CONTRIBUTE/THINGS THAT PERPLEX ME

Although I love my life and unequivocally stand by my decision not to reproduce, I would be lying if I said it doesn't feel lonely sometimes, especially working in an environment where the majority of my colleagues are mothers (and fathers). At one point, several of my coworkers were pregnant simultaneously. Now, in all seriousness, I was happy for each and every one of them. Their kids are extremely cute, and they are content with their choices to become mothers; however, each day at lunch for several months, the excited, nervous moms-to-be prattled on about nesting, signs of labor, and all the things they were looking forward to once their babies arrived. The other women who had older children would share "knowing looks" and winks across the table. They were the veterans that had been through the war and survived to tell about it. I'd sit there eating my peanut butter and jelly sandwich quietly listening to their baby-centered conversations and politely smile and nod. I obviously had nothing to contribute. I completely understand that they were excited about the next chapter in life, but I did feel slightly excluded. Once in a blue moon, someone would throw me a lifeline and ask, "So, how are your dogs doing?" It was a nice attempt to get me involved in the conversation, but a bit awkward too.

Not only did I not have the experience or knowledge to interject anything of value into the baby conversations, but most kid-related things honestly perplex me. For instance, when asked the question, "How old is your child" why must mothers respond in months for such an extended period of time? I've heard so many moms say things like, "I can't believe my little one will be eighteen months next week!" Why not just say, "He's almost a year and a half?" Is it a technique to convince parents that time isn't progressing as quickly? Does it make them feel better in some way to measure their children's ages in months as opposed to years? I just don't understand.

I also feel like I need a Doctorate degree to navigate the complex world of children's clothing sizes. My husband and I used to attempt to buy clothes for our nieces and nephews for holidays, but we were just clueless as to how the crazy system works. What the heck is a 0M, or a 2T, or a 6X? We would inevitably give up, feeling like failures, and buy stuffed animals instead. Those are always the right size.

40. "MOM FRIENDS"

Another phenomenon that mystifies me is the idea of "mom friends." This term has recently seeped into society and every time I hear it, I pause for a moment. I understand that we're often drawn to people because we have things in common. I love that there's a network of parents out there that have become allies. They can share in the joys and support each other through the tribulations of parenthood, but is that the only reason you're friends? I'm fairly certain it's not, but people tend to focus on it. I don't know why, the term just makes me smirk. I mean, my husband sometimes refers to friends of mine from work as my "teacher friends." People will also say, "I'm getting together with my college friends this weekend." I'm used to certain labels for those with whom we socialize, but the "mom friends" category just makes me think that these women are friends solely due to the fact that they all pushed babies forth from their wombs - that that in itself is enough for someone to become close. Because they both procreated, even though they may have nothing else in common, they are now friends for life. I guess I just don't refer to my friends that also have dogs as my "canine owner friends."

I also feel like "mom friends" have a different set of rules. I can recall one pregnant colleague passing another pregnant colleague in the hallway as she exclaimed, "Oh my God! Your bump is so cute!" Now, as "mom friends," they can get away with saying things like this. If I, a childfree woman in her forties had said that, I feel like it would have been a little bit disturbing. There's just an alternative code that moms follow. I'll never break it. I'll never

decipher it. I'll never belong to this secret society,
but I'm at peace with that.

41. "UNTIL YOU ARE A MOTHER..."

As a woman that has not ever, nor will ever
have a little bundle of joy, one phrase that greatly
upsets me is, "Until you are a mom, you will
never..." especially when it's concluded with "know
what it is truly like to love someone." Come again?
Because I didn't grow a tiny human inside of my
uterus, I don't have the capacity to love my spouse as
much as you love yours? Is my love for my parents,
siblings, nieces, nephews, aunts, uncles, cousins, and
friends somehow diminished because I decided not to
have offspring? I find this statement offensive. I'll
grant you that having a child must create a certain
kind of love. That I understand. The bond must be
special and unique. I don't know exactly what it's
like, because I didn't carry on my genepool. I'm sure
it's different than other types of love you've
experienced. I merely dislike the fact that some view
it as the supreme classification of love.

PART J: ATYPICAL TRAITS AND FEELINGS

42. LACK OF MATERNAL INSTICT

During the process of interviewing my "non-mom" friends, I continually discovered that there were several of our experiences that overlapped. We knew early on that we differed from other women. We've observed that certain feelings or desires are just not present in us. The one that was most often mentioned was the lack of genuine "maternal instinct." Many of us realize that we have never possessed that, at least not in the standard way. A close friend of mine shared, "Call it what you will, but I just don't have it. I realized it, embraced it, and there was no sense in trying to force it." She went on to reveal that she just doesn't find babies appealing. When she sees a newborn, she doesn't feel any special tug on her heartstrings.

None of us has ever experienced "baby fever." Not once did I ever feel any kind of desire kick in to reproduce even when all of my friends that were my age began having children. If anything, seeing what they went through cemented the fact that I had definitely made the right choice for me. A former student shares her views as well: "I lacked a natural inclination towards kids. I have no problem with other people's, but the idea of having them did not provide me with fulfillment or excitement. I just know what is not for me, and becoming a parent was never something I aspired to." I think she beautifully expressed many of our feelings.

Some of us also don't seem to have the ability to see that special "glow" that pregnant women supposedly possess. Maybe that's because we'll never have it or feel it. For whatever reason, we can't seem to recognize it. For example, when she sees a woman that is expecting, a friend of mine stated that her initial thought is, "Thank God, that's not me." That comment made me chuckle, because I can completely relate. I'm so thankful I reached out and found all of these women that are so similar to me. If I had never asked, these commonalities would have remained forever hidden and that would have been a great loss.

43. KIDS ARE KIND OF GROSS

Most women that become moms seem to have an ability to overlook the germs, messes, and mysterious stickiness that kids tend to possess. Again, my friends and I lack these moms' aptitude for disgusting situations. One of my former students made me laugh when she sent me a message that echoes my own sentiment. She wrote, "I find kids can be… 'icky.'" I agree with her there. I recall another early sign that kids were not in the cards for me when my sister was again visiting with my niece. She was probably around two at the time, with beautiful curly hair and rosy cheeks. She was gleefully jumping on my bed, despite having a cold that created the lovely strip of green goo under her nostrils that kids that age get from not being able to blow their noses properly. All of a sudden, she exclaimed, "Let's get snuggly!" and proceeded to face plant onto my freshly laundered pillow case! Despite her cuteness and the love I have for her, my initial thought was, "Oh gross! Now I have to wash my sheets again!"

I had a similar encounter with a little cutie when I was in the waiting room of the mechanic. This munchkin was just learning to pull herself up onto things. As her mother's face was illuminated by her cell phone screen, the mini human came over to me and pulled herself up using my legs for assistance. I was just thinking as I mistakenly bent my head a bit to her level, "OK, she is pretty cute..." when all of a sudden, while we were almost face to face, she let out an unobstructed sneeze! I know she had not yet learned the manners of covering her nose and mouth when she sneezed, but come on!

44. FEELING AWKWARD AROUND CHILDREN

Another common trait among those of us with no kids is that we don't feel completely comfortable around them. Again, going back to my "doll-free" childhood, I never even wanted to pretend to be someone's mom, let alone fill the role for real. Some women admitted to me that they think they lack the compassion and patience it would take to be a good mom. Many of us don't naturally know what to do or say around children. Some of us have age groups with which we feel much more at ease. For instance,

I can relate to teenagers more because I can talk to them. After twenty-two years of being a high school teacher, I understand them. I don't have to live with one under my own roof to know that they can be impulsive and moody one day and hilarious and sweet the next. Some folks have a penchant for working with the elderly. While other people are introverts and prefer not to work with or associate with a large number of people of any age. Our comfort levels with other individuals are all different, and that's perfectly fine.

45. FULL LIFE

Civilization has helped to perpetuate this idea of women finding complete fulfillment in becoming mothers. It seems to be considered the ultimate role you can play in your life. There was actually a commercial for a pregnancy test that claimed that the question, "Am I pregnant?" was *the* most important question in a woman's life. This ad irritates me. While I agree that for some, being a mom is their number one role, that's not true of all women. I wish that the alternative would be recognized and discussed more often. Women like me never even seem to be a consideration.

I can assure you, females without children live fulfilling and complete lives, just as those with children do. In our childfree worlds, there's nothing missing. We're not longing for anything. We didn't feel the need to "complete the puzzle." Our jobs, friends, other family members, pets, hobbies, and volunteer work are more than enough to keep us content. Our choices have made us happy, just as motherhood has made other women happy.

46. SIMPLY A FEELING

While many of the women that contributed their thoughts and experiences to this book had a long list of concrete reasons why they are not mothers, a few had a beautifully uncomplicated answer: they simply had a feeling that it was the right call for them. One young woman said, "It's weird because I haven't thought about why I'm childfree. It just sort of has happened and felt right." Another woman phrased it this way: "[It's] just a gut feeling that says, 'I don't want that; I want these things instead.'" Both of these comments struck me as being honest, genuine, and admirable.

I think we should all listen to our inner voices in life more often than we currently do. On occasion they whisper to us and at other times they scream. Sometimes we heed their warnings and follow their advice. Periodically we pretend not to hear the message. I think with something as life-altering as becoming a parent, if you have even the faintest feeling of uncertainty, that sentiment should be honored, even if it's not widely understood.

PART K: INEQUITY

47. TAX BREAKS

Come on, why can't we claim our puppy as a dependent? In addition to the Child Tax Credit, there really should be a Canine Tax Credit. We provide him with food, shelter, toys, supplies, medication, medical care, and yes, even an education of sorts – obedience classes count, right? Over the years, my husband and I have probably spent close to the equivalent of at least one year of college on our pets and their needs, yet we receive no tax breaks. I fully support the fact that parents should be entitled to certain exemptions, but again, someone please throw a bone (pun intended) to those of us that don't get that extra economic assistance each year.

(As I was writing this section of the book, I did happen to see that it has recently been proposed to raise the maximum earned income tax credit for couples without children. My hope is that this change does indeed come to fruition.)

48. WORKPLACE INEQUITY

I'm speaking from my personal experience, but I feel those of us that aren't parental figures also need more equal treatment in the workplace. For example, when I first began teaching, the school's former contract contained a very short list of reasons that we could get personal days approved. Almost all of them were child-centered. I agree that parents need and should have certain accommodations made. However, I would love to see employees without kids receive similar consideration. For instance, one of the reasons on the list was "to attend your child's school event" and I often thought of how many of my niece's school events I would've liked to have been present at over the years.

I've also felt that those of us who are non-parents are expected to take on extra tasks, such as advising clubs or heading committees. Others tend to think, "Well, she can do it. She doesn't have kids. What else could she possibly have going on?" Maybe this is an imagined perception, but it certainly feels like my reality.

There are many times when someone will stand up and excuse themselves early from a meeting because they have to pick their young child up from daycare or at the bus stop. Again, I completely understand this issue. However, when I do the same, let's say because I have to bring my mother to a dentist appointment, I sense that it's looked upon differently. Mothers and fathers never seem to be questioned, but I feel like I constantly have to explain myself and fight for more equal treatment. It's exhausting and disheartening. Everyone in life has their own unique responsibilities and they should be viewed as equally important.

49. "SO SAD... HE WAS THE FATHER OF FOUR..."

As an educator in the twenty-first century, one of the necessary evils that we have to endure is having a safety protocol in case of an active shooter in the building. Nothing brings your mortality into crystal clear focus like being crouched down on the floor of your darkened classroom while you attempt to keep twenty-three other people's kids silent. Although they have fortunately all been practice drills to date, the thought that one day it could become reality kicks in and adrenaline surges. You can't help but wonder, "What would I do if this were an actual threat?" No one can know for certain how they would definitely act in any given situation, especially one that may be fatal, but I would like to think that I would protect not only my students, but also my colleagues at all costs. I've even considered that I'd take more risks because if anything were to happen, I don't have any young, dependent children waiting for me at home. Therefore, while I have even felt this way myself, it doesn't hurt any less that people tend to express a deeper level of sadness when someone passes if they leave kids behind. And, again, this point I do understand, but it still stings.

When watching the news, if there's a story about a police officer that was killed in the line of duty, the anchors never fail to mention, "She was the mother of three" and a certain extra layer of sorrow sets in. Or if a pedestrian was struck and killed, they share that, "He leaves behind a wife and their four children." As an empath, I become deeply upset whenever I hear about another living thing suffering in any way. I constantly grieve for people I don't personally know. I mourn for anyone that loses their life and the family they leave behind, but will my end be any less sad because I don't have kids? "She is survived by her husband and their puppy" honestly doesn't pack the same emotional punch that it would if I had left kids without a mom. I think, as a society, we tend to put more value on parents' lives. This is a tough one for me, as I said, because to a certain extent, I get it. It just still pains me to think that the loss of my life or that of my husband might not be grieved as much by others because we're childfree. OK, this is getting too heavy. Let's bring this to a close.

50. ACCEPTANCE

Whatever the reasons for choosing to be childfree, my hope is that the decision will become more widely accepted if not respected. Folks don't fully understand it, just as we don't fully comprehend wanting to be a parent. I just wish those of us who are childfree could live our lives with less judgment. I recognize that many people unfortunately face all kinds of discrimination each day for a variety of reasons. In no way am I equating the feeling of not being accepted as a childfree woman to the many other much more blatant and painful kinds of prejudice. I realize that the negative reactions we may face from society are minute in comparison to what others experience. This is simply a sharing of my own personal journey and some others like me. I believe we could all benefit from more love, acceptance, support, and kindness, no matter what our differences are.

One of my goals has always been to try my best to support and accept others. We all walk unique paths and although the similarities are what sometimes draw us to one another, the differences are what keep the world interesting. I know our decisions are not the traditional ones, but that's shifting. More and more people are deciding that parenthood is not for them.

For the readers of this book that are parents, I hope you learned something in the previous pages about those of us that have chosen an alternative lifestyle to yours and can appreciate our way of thinking and living a bit more. For those of you like me, I hope that I've helped to confirm your own decision to not have children if that is your wish and have shown you that you are not alone. Consider me one of your "non-mom friends."

OTHER HELPFUL RESOURCES

There are a variety of available resources about being childfree. There are countless groups on social media; however, there's a wide range of personal feelings of the members that join. You may have to research a few before you find a good fit. Do your due diligence before committing to any group, but here are some places to start:

Best Childfree Life Possible – a private Facebook group for people that wish to share the positive aspects of living their best lives without kids; the focus of the posts are people's goals and dreams and no rants are allowed
https://www.facebook.com/groups/bestchildfree/

Childfree – a public Facebook group for people that are childfree by choice
https://www.facebook.com/groups/2204852343/

Childfree and Loving It! – a private Facebook group that is a safe place to vent about childfree issues in a polite way
https://www.facebook.com/Childfreealways/

Respectfully Childfree – a private Facebook group for people that celebrate being childfree in a respectful manner; no derogatory comments about parents or children are permitted on this site
https://www.facebook.com/respectfullychildfree/

There are also many books available on the subject of being childfree. The following books can be found on Amazon or goodreads:

Blackstone, Dr. Amy. *Childfree by Choice: The Movement Redefining Family and Creating a New Age of Independence.* New York: Dutton Books, 2019.

Drut-Davis, Marcia. *What?! You Don't Want Children? Overcoming Rejection in the Childfree Lifestyle.* Austin, TX: Atmosphere Press, 2020.

Williams, Tanya. *A Childfree Happily Ever After: Why More Women are Choosing Not to Have Children.* Melbourne: Grammar Factory Pty. Ltd., 2018.

READ OTHER
50 THINGS TO KNOW
BOOKS

50 Things to Know

Stay up to date with new releases on Amazon:

https://amzn.to/2VPNGr7

CZYKPublishing.com

50 Things to Know

We'd love to hear what you think about our content! Please leave your honest review of this book on Amazon and Goodreads. We appreciate your positive and constructive feedback. Thank you.

Printed in Great Britain
by Amazon